Take Each Day
ONE STEP AT
A TIME

Life is Beautiful!

Enjoy Reading

This book has been donated by

Doris Dillon

July 2001

Take Each Day ONE STEP AT A TIME

Poems to Inspire
and Encourage
the Journey to Recovery

A collection
from Blue Mountain Arts®

Blue Mountain Press ®

Boulder, Colorado

Library of Congress Catalog Card Number: 94-34185
ISBN: 0-88396-395-7

ACKNOWLEDGMENTS appear on page 64.

□ design on book cover is registered in U.S. Patent and Trademark Office.

Manufactured in the United States of America
First Printing: September, 1994

Library of Congress Cataloging-in-Publication Data

Take each day one step at a time : poems to inspire and encourage the
    journey to recovery : a collection from Blue Mountain Arts.
            p.   cm.
        ISBN 0-88396-395-7 : $7.95
            1. Self-actualization (Psychology)—Poetry. 2. American poetry—
    20th century. I. Blue Mountain Arts (Firm)
    PS595.S45T35   1994
    811'.008—dc20   94-34185
                                                                CIP

This book is printed on fine quality, laid embossed, 80 lb. paper. This paper has been specially produced to be acid free (neutral pH) and contains no groundwood or unbleached pulp. It conforms with all of the requirements of the American National Standards Institute, Inc., so as to ensure that this book will last and be enjoyed by future generations.

Blue Mountain Press ®

P.O. Box 4549, Boulder, Colorado 80306

CONTENTS

In the
Difficult Times,
Keep Believing in Yourself

There are times in life
when things are not perfect,
when problems seem to surround you.
As you look for a way through them,
it's important to keep
a positive attitude about your life
and where you are going.
You may wonder if you're making
the right choices.
You may wonder about how things
will turn out
if you take a different road.
But you are a strong
and motivated individual
who will rise to meet
the challenges that face you.
You are a loving and warm person
who loves life,
and you will get through
the difficult times.

— Beverly A. Chisley

Take Things One Day at a Time

*As you begin your journey to recovery,
know that there are people with you
every step of the way.
Take just one day at a time.
Don't expect more from yourself
than you do from others.
Conquer any anger or frustration
with hope and determination.
Believe in yourself.
Believe you will win this battle
and emerge better and stronger than ever.
Fight pain and self-doubt
with prayer and humor.
Reach out and accept the love and support
of your family and friends.
Know that you will overcome this obstacle
as you have all others.*

— Ronnie M. Janney

In time, you will smile again
   and truly feel it,
and your laughter will be genuine.
But until your pain has gone away,
and your sadness has disappeared,
   don't feel you have to be strong.
What you're feeling is real.
Don't feel like you're wrong
   if you want to cry.

There are some roads in life
that we must travel alone,
even though we may be
surrounded by people whom we love.
Some things in life,
   such as what you're feeling now,
can't be felt by anyone but you.

But just remember
you are not alone at all;
everyone who loves you
is walking with you in spirit,
and will be there with you.
You'll find a new strength,
a new peace, and a new happiness.
It just takes a little time.

— *Laurie Wymer*

"Words of Wisdom"

Sometimes the paths we take are long and hard, but remember: those are always the ones that lead to the most beautiful views · Challenges come along, inevitably; how you respond to them determines who you are – deep down inside – and everything you're going to be · Increase the chances of reaching your goals by working at them gradually · The very best you can do is all that is asked of you · Realize that you are capable of working miracles of your own making · Remember that it's up to you to find the key that unlocks the door to a more fulfilling life · Understand that increased difficulty brings you nearer to the truth of how to survive it – and get beyond it · Cross your bridges · Meet your challenges · Reach out for your dreams, and bring them closer and closer to your heart · Get rid of the "if only's," and get on with whatever you need to do to get things right in your life ·

— Collin McCarty

This Can Be a
Time of Growth

As difficult as this time in your life
   may be,
you will become stronger if you
face each day with patience and hope;
if you accept your weaknesses
but concentrate on your strengths;
if you love and care for yourself
even when you are angry and confused;
if you can look at doubt and fear
but keep your mind on the fact that
the struggle is helping you to grow
   in faith and confidence.
If you gently
pick yourself up when you fall
and continue walking;
if you keep thinking about
all the things you can do well,
all the things that bring you joy,
and all the people you love
   who also love you;
if you hold on to your goals
even though the way to reach them
   may be unclear, then...

You can see the troubling times
almost as friends who have come
to help you grow further
than you thought you could;
friends who are showing you the way
to a more courageous heart;
friends who help you to see that
you are more powerful than
you ever thought you were;
friends who help you to see that
the hard times are making you more open
to accepting life as it comes,
and realizing that you have
the inner strength and loving nature
to deal successfully with
any difficult moment.

— *Donna Levine*

The First Step You Take
Is Always
the Most Important One

The first few steps you take
on any journey
won't get you where you want to go.
But without those first steps
and the many more that follow,
you would always be standing
right where you are,
looking towards the future
and wondering what it would
really be like
to see your world
the way you always
dreamed it could be.

One of the greatest lessons
in life is the one you learn
about moving forward
and taking steps to reach your goals.
Life rewards those who are willing
to be involved in it
and take chances.
Take your chance
and take those first few steps,
because a better life is just waiting
for you.

— Nick Santana

You are beginning a personal journey.
At times you may expect the answers to
come quickly, but try to be patient;
some answers may take a lifetime to be
revealed to you.

Though you may be a little uncertain now
and your confidence may be shaken,
you will stand on your own feet soon enough.
Your legs will grow to be strong under you;
they will take you where you want to go.

You'll make mistakes along the way;
a fork in the road may present a path that
you later decide was the wrong way to go.
Take the time to learn from your mistakes,
but don't be too hard on yourself.

You are learning to make your own choices,
and there is great joy in that.
You are a human being who is embarking
on the important journey of discovering
who you are and what you have to offer.
Celebrate your uniqueness, and you will
triumph on your life's journey.

— Deborah Weinberg

The Past Is Past, but Tomorrow Will Last Forever

Our lives have so many
backward glances in them...
thinking back to how things
were and how things might
   have been.

There's nothing wrong with
thinking back, but it probably is
a mistake to dwell on
   the past "what if's."
Instead, we should concentrate
on today, on tomorrow,
and on the tomorrows yet to be.

There are a lot of beautiful days
   yet to come.
The past is past...
   but tomorrow will last forever.

Let each tomorrow
fill your heart with love
   and laughter,
your days with dreams come true,
   and your life with so much
      happiness to look forward to.

— A. Rogers

When You Need Some Help
to Get Through the Day...

When nothing is going right.
When you're wondering, "What
    did I do to deserve this?"
When the day is a disaster,
and a little serenity
    is just what you're after.
When you need a whole lot less
    to concern you,
and a whole lot more to smile about.
When a few peaceful hours
    would seem like a vacation to you,
and you're wondering if there's anything
    you've got to look forward to...

Sometimes you just have to remember:

    It <u>really is</u> going to be okay.
    You're going to make it
        through this day.
    Even if it's one step at a time.

Sometimes you just have to be
    patient and brave and strong.
If you don't know how, just
    make it up as you go along.
And hold on to your hope as though it
    were a path to follow
        or a song you love to sing.

Because if you have hope,
    you have everything.

— Collin McCarty

*Hope is not the closing of your eyes
to the difficulty, the risk,
or the failure.*

*It is a trust that —
if I fail now —
I shall not fail forever;
and if I am hurt,
I shall be healed.*

*It is a trust that
life is good,
love is powerful,
and the future is full of promise.*

— *Anonymous*

The Serenity Prayer

God grant me the serenity
to accept the things
  I cannot change;
the courage to change
  the things I can;
and the wisdom
  to know the difference.

— Reinhold Niebuhr

Peace and Happiness
Must Come from Within

Whatever a person becomes
on the outside
must first be believed
in the heart.
We all become different people
as we grow older,
with different hopes and dreams,
goals and achievements,
memories and feelings.
No one can ever say that, as a person,
they are all they can be,
for it is then that they
have stopped growing from within.

In a time of new beginnings,
continue to grow, to dream,
and to make new memories.
Whatever gives you peace
within yourself
will allow others to see
the special person you truly are.

— Shirley Vander Pol

*Sometimes admitting our weaknesses
is the bravest thing we can do.
Because with that admission,
we drop our shield of pretense,
find the courage to face reality,
and reach out for the help we need.*

*They say that the first step
on the road to recovery
is the hardest.
But while the road
is not always an easy one,
recovery offers you a new chance
to learn to love yourself,
your family, and life.
It takes time to get adjusted
to a new way of living
and to learn to enjoy
the peacefulness that recovery offers.
There will be times
when you will feel anxious,
and that's normal.
But you deserve to live in love
and happiness,
and there is no greater gift
you could give yourself.*

— Donna Newman

You will be whatever you resolve to be. Determine to be something in the world, and you will be something.

"I cannot," never accomplished anything.

But "I will try," has worked wonders.

— *Joel Hawes*

Recovery Is a Learning Process

Recovery is about learning to love and value yourself enough to stop destroying yourself. It's about learning to change your mind and your heart. It's about forgiving yourself and others. It's about letting go of shame and learning to accept your true self.

Recovery is about letting go of the lofty expectation of perfection that you have placed upon yourself and others. It's learning to love and accept yourself and others unconditionally.

Recovery is about learning to use your anger as the fuel to create something good, rather than denying it or holding it inside until you self-destruct or strike out at another.

Recovery is about learning that you have a choice: You can choose to be hopeful rather than hopeless; you can choose to act from faith rather than react from fear; and you can choose to enjoy life rather than merely survive it.

— *Donna Newman*

Peace Is Coming

Rest assured
that peace is at hand.
The time is coming
when all of your
self-built walls
and guarded halls
will wither to dust.

The free-flowing love
of your spirit within
soon will be released
to love
and, as it has been your
desire from birth,
to find a spirit
who will not chain you
or claim you
as a possession,
who will not crush
your inner being
as a flower is crushed
by an unfaithful hand.

Rest assured
that the time is coming
for you simply
to share,
to grow,
to learn,
to love.

— L. Dale Cox

I'm Finally Learning to Just Be "Me," and It Feels Wonderful

Ever since I can remember,
I've been a codependent person.
I always tried my hardest
to please other people.
When it came to others' feelings,
I would put them before my own—
even if it meant
sacrificing my own needs.
I cared too much about
what others thought of me.
I tried to be everyone's friend.
I was a "people pleaser":
doing, saying, and being
whatever everyone else
wanted me to be.
I lost out on knowing who I really was.
It reached the point where
I didn't even know what I wanted in life.
I was unable
to make even simple decisions,
because in a way,
I had lost my true identity.

I'm still a codependent person—
but now I'm a recovering one.
I recognize my weaknesses,
and because I can now put myself first—
before everyone else—
I can finally be "me."

— Sherée Heller

Only You Know
What Is Best for You

You cannot listen to what
others want you to do
You must listen to yourself
Society
family
friends
do not know what
you must do
Only you know
and only you
can do what is
right for you
So start right now
You will need to
work very hard
You will need to
overcome many obstacles
You will need to go
against the better
judgment of many people
and you will need to
bypass their prejudices
But you can have
whatever you want
if you try hard enough
So start right now and
you will live
a life designed
by you and
for you
and you will
love
your
life

— Susan Polis Schutz

Share Your Feelings with Someone Who Will Understand

Good or bad, feelings need expression;
they must be recognized and given
freedom to reveal themselves.
It isn't wise to hide behind a smile
when your heart is breaking;
that is not being true to how
you feel inside.
By letting out your feelings,
your pain is released,
and you are able to go on —
to reconstruct your life and
think of other things
that will make you happy again.

Put away the myth that says
you must be strong enough to face
the whole world with a smile and
a brave attitude all of the time.
You have your feelings that say otherwise,
so admit that they are there.
Use their healing power
to put the past behind you,
and realize that those expressive
stirrings in your heart
are very much a part of you.
Use them to get better,
to find peace within,
to be true to yourself.

— Barbara J. Hall

Be Kind to Yourself...

There will always be times
when it's hard to remember
your strengths.
These are the times
when you need
to give yourself special attention.
Be kind to yourself...
Kindness nurtures
and gives hope
to growing dreams.
Respect yourself...
Listen to your needs,
and treat yourself
as you would a friend.
Encourage yourself...
Remember what you truly want,
and fight for it
as you would your life.
Appreciate yourself...
Don't take for granted
the qualities
that make you unique.
Focus yourself...
It is with discipline
and motivation
that you will move towards your goals.
Be giving towards yourself...
In that way, your strength will thrive,
and you'll be realizing your goals
a day at a time.

— Gail Mutterperl

The Ghosts in Our Lives

Our lives are filled with ghosts
Skeleton ties
To people we have loved
Their shadows reappear
When memory breathes life into them
Shades of our parents
Impressions of old lovers
We paint anew
On the faces of strangers and friends
That enter our lives
Our ghosts
They visit us again and again
Until we learn
What they have come to teach us
And we master the puzzle that
We are partners in
We wrestle with our ghosts
Until we put them to sleep
Silence them
By listening to them at last

— Parvene Michaels

Detachment

We are all attached
in some way
to the baggage of the past or the
desires of our hearts and minds for tomorrow.

The umbilical cords that connect each of us
to these empty and artificial times
grow thicker with every passing
day and subsequent event.

We must all learn to detach from
the demands and pulls of the unknown
and our concern for the past.

To detach
is to let go, not of the thing
but of the need for the thing.

To detach
is to let go of the dependency on a person,
but to hold on to the preference
for the person.

To detach
is to let go of the habit, not the
desire for the pleasure of the outcome.

To detach
is to release the old you
and embrace the new you.

— *Tim Connor*

Autobiography in Five Short Chapters
by Portia Nelson

Chapter I

I walk down the street.
There is a deep hole in the sidewalk.
I fall in.
I am lost... I am hopeless.
It isn't my fault.
It takes forever to find a way out.

Chapter II

I walk down the same street.
There is a deep hole in the sidewalk.
I **pretend** I don't see it.
I fall in again.
I can't believe I am in this same place.
But it isn't my fault.
It still takes a long time to get out.

Chapter III

I walk down the same street.
There is a deep hole in the sidewalk.
I **see** it there.
I still fall in... it's a habit... but,
my eyes are open.
I know where I am.
It is **my** fault.
I get out immediately.

Chapter IV

I walk down the same street.
There is a deep hole in the sidewalk.
I walk around it.

Chapter V

I walk down another street.

"My Focus Is on Wellness"

...An Affirmation for Healing and Recovery

*E*ach day, each minute, is
no longer a struggle.
Somehow, my body is now free.
I can sit in silence and focus
on my breathing.
I am no longer distracted.
My body is now working
for me, not against me.

My mind is now experiencing
a serenity I have never known before.
I have developed an inner strength
that carries me through
even the most difficult times.
I can now focus on my goals
and desires.

Every experience of my life
is somehow new again.
My senses are more acute
than ever before.
I find pleasure in every task,
no matter how routine it is.

There is a place of healing
inside me now
where I feel as if I am standing
on a beach covered with
  crystal-white sand,
surrounded by sparkling blue water.
I feel the sand between my toes
and the sun beaming down on my back.
I stand near the water
and the tides seem
  to reach towards me,
but I am now flowing with the currents
and not against them.

— Marcy Perlmutter

A New Strength

*There are times in every life
when we feel hurt or alone...
But I believe that these times
when we feel lost
and all around us seems
   to be falling apart
   are really bridges of growth.
We struggle and try to recapture
   the security of what was,
   but almost in spite of ourselves,
   we emerge on the other side
   with a new understanding,
     a new awareness,
     a new strength.
   It is almost as though
     we must go through the pain
     and the struggle
       in order to grow
   and reach new heights.*

— Sue Mitchell

Be True to Yourself,
No Matter What

Right now, you are struggling
    with your inner world.
You are asking yourself
    how you feel about everything
and if you are really happy.
You are changing into
    the exact person
that you were hoping to become,
but now you find that these changes
    are causing difficulties
for the people around you.
They want you to remain
    the same person that you've been;
they may even want you to be
    something for them
rather than being yourself.
But now is the time to make
    a statement about your life.
You must continue to follow
    your own chosen path
and make alterations in
    your lifestyle.

You will find your new place
    in the circle of your loved ones,
but keep in mind that
everyone must create their own
    sense of self and happiness.
No one should be shaped or confined
by someone else's ideals of
    what they should be.
Strive for your own beliefs
    and desires;
continue to make your world complete
by being yourself.
Every day, discover something
    new and unique about yourself,
and remember that happiness
    and contentment in life
come when you focus on
    your own goals,
being yourself, and making the most of
every minute of your life.

— Dena Dilaconi

Beginning Today...

Today
look in a mirror
and notice
that the person
who greets you
is beautiful,
inside and out.

Today
say to yourself that
you know nothing is
impossible.
Remind yourself that
every one of your dreams
is within reach.

Today
think about all of
the people who love you,
who see the beauty in you,
and begin to look at yourself
in the same way.

— Lise Schlosser

Have Faith...

Faith begins
by believing
in your heart
that what is right
has a chance.

It is knowing
in your heart
that good can
overcome evil,
that the sun can shine
after a rainstorm.

Faith is peaceful
and comforting;
it comes from within
where no one
can invade
your private dreams.

*Faith is not something
you can demand or command;
it is a commitment
to a belief.*

*Faith is believing
in something that
you cannot see or hear,
something deep inside
that only you understand
and control.*

*Faith is trusting
in yourself
enough to know
that no matter
how things turn out,
you will make
the best of them.*

— Beth Fagan Quinn

May You Find Serenity

May you find serenity and tranquility in a world you may not always understand. May the pain you have known and the conflict you have experienced give you the strength to walk through life facing each new situation with courage and optimism. Always know that there are those whose love and understanding will always be there, even when you feel most alone. May a kind word, a reassuring touch, and a warm smile be yours every day of your life, and may you give these gifts as well as receive them. Realize that what you feel you lack in one regard may be more than compensated for in another. What you feel you lack in the present may become one of your strengths in the future. May you see your future as one filled with promise and possibility. Learn to view everything as a worthwhile experience. May you find enough inner strength to determine your own worth by yourself, and not be dependent on another's judgment of your accomplishments. May you always feel loved.

— Sandra Sturtz Hauss

What You Are Doing
Takes Real Courage

Courage is the feeling that you can make it,
no matter how challenging the situation.
It is knowing that you can reach out
for help and you are not alone.
Courage is accepting each day,
knowing that you have the inner resources
to deal with the ordinary things
as well as the confusing things,
with the exciting things
as well as the painful things.
Courage is taking the time
to get involved with life, family,
and friends,
and giving your love and energy
in whatever ways you can.

Courage is being who you are,
being aware of your good qualities
and talents,
and not worrying about
what you do not have.
Courage is allowing yourself to live
as fully as you can,
to experience as much of life
as you are able to,
to grow and develop yourself
in whatever directions you need to.
Courage is having hope for the future
and trust in the natural flow of life.
It is being open to change.
Courage is having faith that life
is a beautiful gift.

— Donna Levine

Someone Is Always
There for You

Stressful situations and trying times
  are some of the realities of life.
When you experience them,
  you may think they'll never leave.
But even the most difficult times come and go,
and the strength you need to meet
  the situation
will be there for you in the helping hand
  of a friend,
in the compassion of a loved one
  who cares,
and in the listening ear of someone who knows
  what you're going through.
All you have to do is look up and reach out,
and someone will be there
  to share your troubles.

— Linda E. Knight

My Journey to Recovery

In the beginning,
I wondered if I would
ever make it through.
There were periods of anger,
sadness, pain, and grief;
times when I wondered,
   "Why me?"

But one day,
there was a glimpse of light,
and then another.
The clouds began to break apart,
and I started to see beyond them.
The times when I felt happy and safe
began to outnumber the times
when I felt sad and frightened.
New friendships were formed;
feelings of trust and resolution
began to replace past feelings
of hopelessness and self-doubt.
I seemed to emerge from the darkness
into the light with a new sense
of empowerment.

*I now realize that there are things
about my past that I cannot change,
but I can stop them from controlling
my life and my happiness.
I know that this part of my life
will never go away entirely,
but it has begun to take a less
prominent place in my existence.
I have begun to allow other thoughts
to enter my mind,
and I have a better understanding
of myself –
my strengths and weaknesses.
I'm not afraid to set limits.
I've begun to enjoy life again
and to think about the future.
I can now look back on this time
for what it was –
a period of growth,
self-discovery,
and healing.*

— Anna Marie Edwards

One Day at a Time

Bridges can be built,
  one day at a time.
Forgiveness can be felt,
  one day at a time.

Balance can be achieved,
  one day at a time.
Dreams can be believed,
lost smiles can be found,
and your most meaningful
  plans can succeed.

New horizons can be reached,
  one day at a time.
The journey inward can be complete,
  one day at a time.
Spiritual meaning can be your guide,
  one day at a time.
Health, healing, and
  happiness thrive...

  one day at a time.

— Alin Austin

24 Things to Always Remember...
and One Thing to Never Forget

Your presence is a present to the world.
You're unique and one of a kind.
Your life can be what you want it to be.
Take the days just one at a time.

Count your blessings, not your troubles.
You'll make it through whatever comes along.
Within you are so many answers.
Understand, have courage, be strong.

Don't put limits on yourself.
So many dreams are waiting to be realized.
Decisions are too important to leave to chance.
Reach for your peak, your goal, your prize.

Nothing wastes more energy than worrying.
The longer one carries a problem,
*   the heavier it gets.*
Don't take things too seriously.
Live a life of serenity, not a life of regrets.

Remember that a little love goes a long way.
Remember that a lot... goes forever.
Remember that friendship is a wise investment.
Life's treasures are people... together.

Realize that it's never too late.
Do ordinary things in an extraordinary way.
Have health and hope and happiness.
Take the time to wish upon a star.

And don't ever forget...
*   for even a day... how very special you are.*

— Collin McCarty

The Sun Will Shine
on You Again

We all know that
no matter how many clouds
get in the way,
the sun keeps on shining.
No matter how many times its rays
are blocked from our view,
the sun will reappear on another day
to shine more brilliantly than before.
It takes determination
to outlast those dark clouds
that sometimes enter your life,
and patience to keep on shining
no matter what gets in your way.
But it all pays off eventually.
One of these days
when you least expect it,
you'll overcome your difficulties,
because you and the sun
have a lot in common:
You're both going to shine
no matter what.

— Barbara J. Hall

ACKNOWLEDGMENTS

The following is a partial list of authors whom the publisher especially wishes to thank for permission to reprint their works.

Ronnie M. Janney for "Take Things One Day at a Time." Copyright © 1994 by Ronnie M. Janney. All rights reserved. Reprinted by permission.

Nick Santana for "The First Step You Take...." Copyright © 1994 by Nick Santana. All rights reserved. Reprinted by permission.

Deborah Weinberg for "You are beginning a personal journey." Copyright © 1994 by Deborah Weinberg. All rights reserved. Reprinted by permission.

Donna Newman for "Sometimes admitting our weaknesses..." and "Recovery Is a Learning Process." Copyright © 1994 by Donna Newman. All rights reserved. Reprinted by permission.

L. Dale Cox for "Peace Is Coming." Copyright © 1994 by L. Dale Cox. All rights reserved. Reprinted by permission.

Sherée Heller for "I'm Finally Learning to Just Be 'Me'...." Copyright © 1994 by Sherée Heller. All rights reserved. Reprinted by permission.

Barbara J. Hall for "Share Your Feelings with Someone Who Will Understand." Copyright © 1994 by Barbara J. Hall. All rights reserved. Reprinted by permission.

Gail Mutterperl for "Be Kind to Yourself...." Copyright © 1994 by Gail Mutterperl. All rights reserved. Reprinted by permission.

Parvene Michaels for "The Ghosts in Our Lives." Copyright © 1994 by Parvene Michaels. All rights reserved. Reprinted by permission.

Tim Connor for "Detachment." Copyright © 1993 by Tim Connor. All rights reserved. Reprinted by permission.

Portia Nelson for "Autobiography in Five Short Chapters." From **There's a Hole in My Sidewalk.** Copyright © 1992 by Portia Nelson. Published by Beyond Words Publishing, Inc., Hillsboro, Oregon. All rights reserved. Reprinted by permission.

Marcy Perlmutter for "My Focus Is on Wellness." Copyright © 1994 by Marcy Perlmutter. All rights reserved. Reprinted by permission.

Dena Dilaconi for "Be True to Yourself, No Matter What." Copyright © 1994 by Dena Dilaconi. All rights reserved. Reprinted by permission.

Lise Schlosser for "Beginning Today...." Copyright © 1994 by Lise Schlosser. All rights reserved. Reprinted by permission.

Beth Fagan Quinn for "Have Faith...." Copyright © 1994 by Beth Fagan Quinn. All rights reserved. Reprinted by permission.

Donna Levine for "What You Are Doing Takes Real Courage." Copyright © 1994 by Donna Levine. All rights reserved. Reprinted by permission.

Linda E. Knight for "Stressful situations and trying times...." Copyright © 1994 by Linda E. Knight. All rights reserved. Reprinted by permission.

A careful effort has been made to trace the ownership of poems used in this anthology in order to obtain permission to reprint copyrighted materials and give proper credit to the copyright owners. If any error or omission has occurred, it is completely inadvertent, and we would like to make corrections in future editions provided that written notification is made to the publisher: BLUE MOUNTAIN PRESS, INC., P.O. Box 4549, Boulder, Colorado 80306.

If you are interested in submitting your original poetry to Blue Mountain Press for possible inclusion in a future anthology, please write for guidelines or send your work with SASE to: BMA Editorial Department, P. O. Box 1007, Dept. BP, Boulder, Colorado 80306.